# CYBER

# CRIME
# SECRETS

John Townsend

amicus

Published by Amicus
P.O. Box 1329
Mankato, MN 56002

Printed in the United States of America at Corporate Graphics, in North Mankato, Minnesota.

Library of Congress Cataloging-in-Publication Data
Townsend, John, 1955-
 Cyber crime secrets / by John Townsend.
     p. cm. -- (Amazing crime scene science)
 Includes bibliographical references and index.
 Summary: "Presents different ways cyber crime is committed and the many ways electronic equipment
can be used to solve crimes. Includes case files and case studies from real cyber crime situations"--Provided by publisher.
 ISBN 978-1-60753-168-5 (library binding)
 1.  Computer crimes--Juvenile literature. 2.  Cyberterrorism--Juvenile literature.  I. Title.
 HV6773.T683 2012
 363.25'968--dc22
                                    2010033805

Appleseed Editions, Ltd.
Created by Q2AMedia
Editor: Katie Dicker
Art Director: Harleen Mehta
Designer: Cheena Yadav
Picture Researcher: Debabrata Sen

All words in **bold** can be found in the Glossary on pages 30–31.

Web site information is correct at the time of going to press. However, the publishers cannot
accept liability for any information or links found on third-party web sites.

Picture credits
t= top, b= bottom, l= left, r= right

Mikkel William Nielsen/Istockphoto: Title page, Rich Legg/Istockphoto: 4, Toria/Shutterstock: 5, Federico Ciamei/
Istockphoto: 6, Carsten Reisinger/Dreamstime: 7, Jon Riley/Stone/Getty Images: 8, Rannev/Shutterstock: 9t, Ho New/Reuters,
Joseph/Shutterstock, Vladm/Shutterstock: 9, Edhar/Shutterstock: 10, Picture Perfect/Rex Features: 11, Chris Gramly/
Istockphoto: 12, Arest/Shutterstock: 13t, Pejo/Shutterstock: 13b, Mikkel William Nielsen/Istockphoto: 14, Slavoljub Pantelic/
Shutterstock: 15t, Luis Louro/Shutterstock: 15b, Chris Jackson/Getty Images: 16, ImageTeam/Shutterstock: 17, Patti Sapone/
AP Images: 18, Jonathan Crellin: 19, Joroma/Shutterstock: 20, India Today Group/Getty Images: 21, Philippe Psaila/
Science Photo Library: 22, Nikhil Gangavane/ Dreamstime: 23, Getty Images News/Getty Images: 24, Handout/
Getty images News/Getty Images: 25, Anyka/Shutterstock: 26, Jose Antonio Sanchez Reyes/Dreamstime: 27,
Izabela Zaremba/Shutterstock: 28, David Hernandez/Dreamstime: 29, ImageTeam/Shutterstock: 31.
Cover images: ImageTeam/Shutterstock, Rich Legg/Istockphoto, Paul/Photolibrary.

DAD0052
3-2011

9 8 7 6 5 4 3 2 1

# CONTENTS

The Digital Age . . . . . . . . . . . . . . . . . . . . . 4

Cyber Vandals . . . . . . . . . . . . . . . . . . . . . 6

Cyber Theft . . . . . . . . . . . . . . . . . . . . . . .8

Spam Scam . . . . . . . . . . . . . . . . . . . . . . 10

Identity Theft . . . . . . . . . . . . . . . . . . . . 12

Terrorism . . . . . . . . . . . . . . . . . . . . . . . 14

Cyber Forensics . . . . . . . . . . . . . . . . . . . 16

Case Study: Clues to a Murder . . . . . . . . 18

GPS Spies . . . . . . . . . . . . . . . . . . . . . . .20

Cell Phone Secrets . . . . . . . . . . . . . . . .22

Case Study: Cell Phone Evidence . . . . . . .24

Catching Criminals . . . . . . . . . . . . . . . .26

What Next? . . . . . . . . . . . . . . . . . . . . .28

Glossary . . . . . . . . . . . . . . . . . . . . . . .30

Index and Web Finder . . . . . . . . . . . . . . 32

# The Digital Age

Modern **forensic** science often involves far more than testing physical **evidence** found at a crime scene. It can include cyber evidence—which is unseen electronic data and digital information.

A computer may be a crime scene, but its effects spread much farther.

## Crime Waves

A crime scene is where a crime has been committed. This may be an obvious place, such as a smashed safe or an abandoned getaway car. But cyber crime is very different. This type of crime involves computers, cell phones, or other electronic equipment, and it can occur anywhere.

Since the 1970s, the growth in technology has brought great advances to everyday life and to the world of crime. Today, some crime scene investigators specialize in **digital forensics**. They trace all kinds of instant messaging and computer-related communications.

## Growing Threats

Cyber crime continues to grow every year, costing huge amounts of money. The Federal Bureau of Investigation (FBI) has a "cyber mission" to tackle:

- serious computer **hacking** and the spread of computer viruses,
- Internet **fraud**,
- online **predators**, and
- actions that affect national security.

Although computers have become major tools for today's criminals, cyber technology also has the power to catch many of these criminals at their own game. This book explains some amazing cyber crime secrets.

### SCIENCE SECRETS

Cyber forensic scientists can extract the memory from laptop computers and cell phones for crime scene evidence. A criminal's call history can reveal details and dates of text messages, e-mails, images, and videos. This information can be used as evidence in **court**.

Computers have brought more crime to the world, but they also help to catch criminals.

# Cyber Vandals

A vandal is someone who damages property. This is a criminal offense in most cases. Cyber vandals deliberately damage computers by spreading computer viruses or faulty software.

Computer hackers damage the software on a computer.

## Serious Assault

Cyber vandals get a sense of power or fame by destroying, changing, or disrupting information on web sites. These attacks may seem fairly harmless, but the effect on some businesses can be serious. A web site that has been tampered with has to be shut down and repaired before it can be used again. If vandals post racial, political, or **obscene** messages on a web site, it may become a crime scene.

## Computer Viruses

A computer virus is a type of **malware**. This software spreads via the Internet and infects computers through e-mails or corrupted web links. The virus infects programs and changes how a computer works, causing damage.

Forms of computer vandalism include:

- **Worms** that copy themselves and spread through computer networks and the Internet

- **Trojans** that claim to do one thing but really do another; They may damage a computer's hard drive or allow a hacker to access a computer system.

- **Spyware** that spies on what a user does on the computer that may reveal secret login codes or passwords

Finding a virus on your computer is bad news.

## Cyber Criminal

In 2005, 17-year-old Sven Jaschan of Germany was given a 21-month **suspended sentence** after being found guilty of cyber vandalism. He had created the Sasser worm, which harmed computers around the world.

# Cyber Theft

Unlike cyber vandals, cyber thieves try to get rich by hacking into computers to steal money or secrets to sell. Some cyber thieves have been teenagers robbing banks while in their own bedrooms!

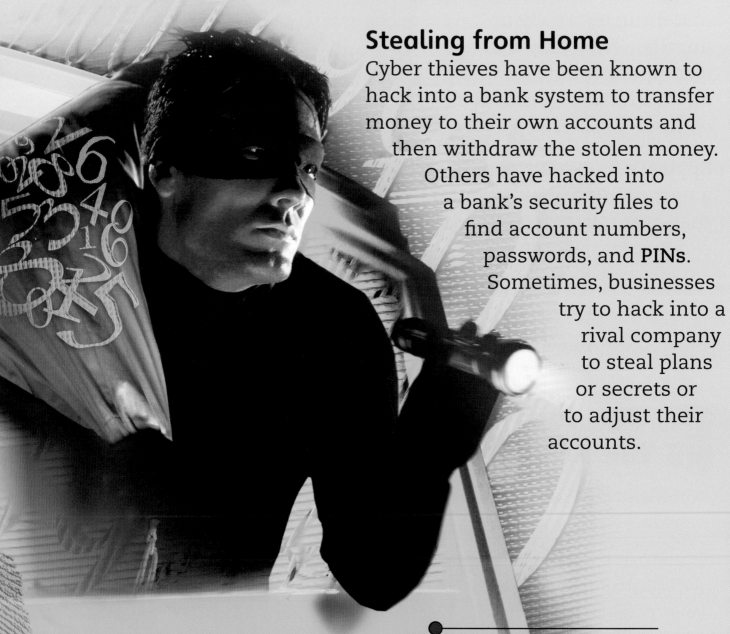

## Stealing from Home

Cyber thieves have been known to hack into a bank system to transfer money to their own accounts and then withdraw the stolen money. Others have hacked into a bank's security files to find account numbers, passwords, and **PINs**. Sometimes, businesses try to hack into a rival company to steal plans or secrets or to adjust their accounts.

Cyber thieves often work undetected.

# CASE FILE

In 2007, the mastermind behind a $20 million cyber theft was an 18-year-old computer whiz kid from New Zealand. He called himself AKILL and spent hours on his home computer every night writing software to allow criminals to access millions of bank accounts. The FBI eventually traced his criminal activities and arrested him.

## CAN YOU BELIEVE IT?

Raphael Gray from Wales was just 19 when he hacked the credit card details of Microsoft founder Bill Gates in 2001. Three years earlier, a 16-year-old and a 17-year-old in California were caught hacking into the computer system at the **Pentagon**.

# CASE FILE

In 2010, 28-year-old Albert Gonzalez was jailed for 20 years for cyber theft. As a teenager in Florida, he used a school computer to hack into the government of India's computer system. But it was hacking into major U.S. businesses that led to his conviction.

Gonzalez is now serving 20 years in prison.

Gonzalez sold millions of customers' account details to other criminals for an estimated $2.8 million, which he used to buy an apartment, a car, Rolex watches, and a $75,000 birthday party. He also buried $1 million cash in his parents' backyard. Gonzalez said he had become addicted to hacking. As the highest earning hacker in history, he now has to find other pastimes in prison.

# Spam Scam

Many cyber theives send e-mails to trick people into revealing private information such as bank card details. These scams, called **phishing**, allow thieves to make **illegal** purchases online.

## E-mail Scams

If an e-mail directs you to a web site that asks for personal details—beware! The web site likely looks real, but it is probably a fake—set up to steal a user's information. Although cyber detectives are on the lookout for such scams and regularly catch the criminals, this type of fraud is on the increase.

Beware of web sites that ask for your personal details. They may be a hoax!

## Junk Mail

**Spammers** send out more than 100 million junk e-mails a day. Many of these e-mails ask people to click links that make phishing attacks a multimillion dollar industry. Criminals try to get victims to download harmful software onto their computers to steal bank account details and passwords.

In 2009, 87 percent of the e-mail messages sent were spam e-mails. The death of Michael Jackson in that year generated the most spam—almost 2 percent of all spam messages.

### DID YOU KNOW?

The United States creates 60 percent of all spam e-mails. China generates the next largest amount of spam. However, scams and fraud account for only about 2 percent of spam e-mail. About 36 percent of junk e-mail is advertising.

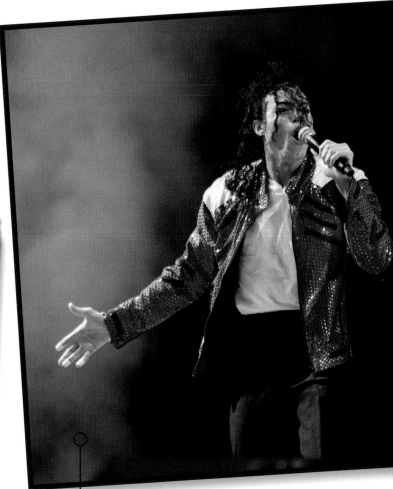

Michael Jackson's death in 2009 created a new wave of spam e-mails.

## World Cup Tricks

Soccer fans were targeted by cyber criminals in the preliminaries to the 2010 World Cup with a series of spam e-mails, fake offers, and attempts to steal bank account details. Those tricked into sending money received nothing in return.

# Identity Theft

Many cyber crimes involve stealing people's personal details for illegal use, entering a country, or causing acts of terrorism. Such identity theft lets a criminal pretend to be someone else.

## Growing Crime

According to experts, every 79 seconds another person becomes a victim of online identity theft. That means many millions of people have already had their private information stolen and used by criminals for illegal purposes. The following two cases from 2008 show how digital forensics caught the identity thieves.

Anyone can be an identity theft criminal if they know how to hack into a computer.

### DID YOU KNOW?

**Bots** are now often used by cyber criminals. They allow hackers to take control of many computers at a time and turn them into zombie computers. These operate as part of a "botnet" to spread viruses, generate spam, and commit other types of online crime and fraud.

# CASE FILE

In 2008, a 16-year-old boy known only as Ajay became an identity thief in Ahmedabad, India. He hacked into web sites and stole customers' numbers and personal details to sell to other criminals. Ajay's tools were his laptop computer and a cell phone. He was careful to cover his tracks, leaving no digital evidence on his own computer. However, the evidence against him came from another gang member who left **incriminating** details on his own computer. Once arrested, Ajay showed the police a few of his tricks and helped them to track down other identity thieves.

Computer fraud can take place in a teenager's bedroom!

# CASE FILE

Bonnie and Clyde were famous bank robbers in the United States in the 1930s. In 2008, another couple became known as the Bonnie and Clyde of identity fraud. Edward Anderton and Jocelyn Kirsch stole personal information from friends, colleagues, and neighbors to pay for an extravagant lifestyle. The couple stole approximately $120,000 from their victims before their computer equipment was seized. Anderton was sent to prison for four years. Kirsch received a five-year sentence because she continued her crimes after being questioned by the police.

# Terrorism

Cyber terrorism involves criminal activities that target national security data. This type of terrorism attacks computer systems and accesses top secret information to cause fear and violence.

## Growing Threats

Cyber terrorism is a rapidly expanding threat. But some cyber terrorists have been caught and convicted because of information stored on their own computers.

## CAN YOU BELIEVE IT?

John Allen Muhammad was executed by lethal injection in 2009 for a string of shootings that terrorized Washington, D.C. in 2002. A laptop computer in his car helped cyber forensics trace his steps. The computer contained key evidence such as a **ransom** note demanding $5 million, code words, and a map of his crime scenes.

Cyber terrorists use their hacking skills to cause fear and violence in different countries of the world.

# CASE FILE

In 2007, Michael Curtis Reynolds of Montana was convicted of cyber terrorist activities. Using the Internet, he involved **Al-Qaeda** in a plot to blow up the Trans-Continental gas pipeline, a Wyoming oil refinery, and the Trans-Alaska oil pipeline. The FBI gathered evidence from his computers and e-mails, which outlined his bomb plans.

Reynolds was arrested by the FBI in 2005 while trying to collect a bag filled with $40,000. He thought the money was being supplied by an Al-Qaeda contact he had met online. During his trial, Reynolds claimed that he was trying to catch terrorists on the Internet to report them to the FBI. But digital evidence proved Reynolds had supplied details of bomb-making equipment for terrorist attacks. He was sentenced to 30 years in prison.

Cyber terrorism is a growing threat, so forensic experts keep track of digital evidence.

# Cyber Forensics

**CSI** officers often look for a **suspect's** computer so that experts can test it for secrets—including deleted information. Usually, they need a **warrant** to search someone's personal property.

## The Search for Clues

Like any investigation, a seized computer must be made secure so no digital information is altered or lost. Computer experts look for files that are **encrypted**, protected by passwords, hidden, or deleted. The files are copied, so the original data remains unchanged. Records are kept to ensure that accurate evidence is used in court.

When a computer is seized, it is wrapped in plastic to preserve fingerprints and other evidence.

# Chat Room Danger

Making friends using online chat rooms can be risky because you never know who you are talking to. Ashleigh Hall, a 17-year-old student from Darlington, UK, agreed to meet a young "friend" she met online. He turned out to be Peter Chapman, a 33-year-old predator. He strangled Ashleigh and left her body in a field.

When digital forensic experts examined Ashleigh's computer, they found Peter Chapman's false identity on the social networking site Facebook. The police arrested him and he was sentenced to life in prison in 2010.

Forensic scientists can find many secrets when they examine the inside of a computer.

## DID YOU KNOW?

Some criminals make it more difficult for investigators to find information on their hard drives by using programs known as anti-forensics. Detectives have to disable these programs to get to the hidden information they need. But with the right software, they can even find deleted files.

# Clues to a Murder

A particularly gruesome killing made headline news in 2007 when a woman went on trial for the murder of her husband. It was mostly computer evidence that sent Melanie McGuire to prison.

## Grim Discovery

In May 2004, a fisherman pulled a suitcase from the Chesapeake Bay in Maryland. He was horrified to find human body parts inside. A week later, two more suitcases containing body parts washed up on a nearby beach. CSI officers were soon trying to identify the victim. He had been shot before his body was cut up.

Within weeks, detectives knew the name of the victim. William McGuire was identified when a sketch of his face was published and recognized by a friend. Very soon, William's wife, Melanie, became the chief suspect in his murder.

Melanie McGuire was put on trial for the murder of her husband William in 2004.

## Vital Evidence

Forensic scientists began linking William's death to the family home in Woodbridge, New Jersey, which they believed to be the murder scene:

- Plastic bags in which the murderer placed William McGuire's body parts were similar to bags found in the McGuire home.

- The suitcases in which William McGuire's body parts were found belonged to the McGuires.

- Melanie McGuire had bought a drug from a local pharmacy just before her husband disappeared.

## Cyber Clues

However, it was the evidence found on Melanie's computer that suggested she drugged her husband before shooting him and disposing of his body. Computer data showed Internet searches for information on drugs, guns, and poisons. Melanie McGuire was sentenced to life in prison.

Computer hard drives containing telltale evidence are examined by cyber experts to find hidden information—even deleted data.

## CAN YOU BELIEVE IT?

Melanie McGuire could not hide the secrets on her computer. Shortly before her husband's murder, searches had included undetectable poisons and methods for committing murder and purchasing guns. One search related to the pharmacy where she purchased a drug using a false name on the morning of the murder.

# GPS Spies

Criminals can use a **GPS device** to locate or escape from a crime scene. This digital information can help forensic detectives trace a criminal's steps.

## Hidden Secrets

Drivers who use GPS devices may not realize they have a spy in their vehicle. Digital information stored on the memory card can reveal where the driver was at a particular time. Details of a suspect's whereabouts at different times, each journey, and addresses of contacts can all be recovered from GPS equipment. The police may find this information very useful!

The GPS system in a car can hold many vital clues to a person's daily journeys.

### DID YOU KNOW?

Digital devices known as event data recorders are now standard equipment in many new cars. They record speed, braking, signaling, or other driving behavior and can show forensic investigators vital details about a crime, a crash, or getaway car chases.

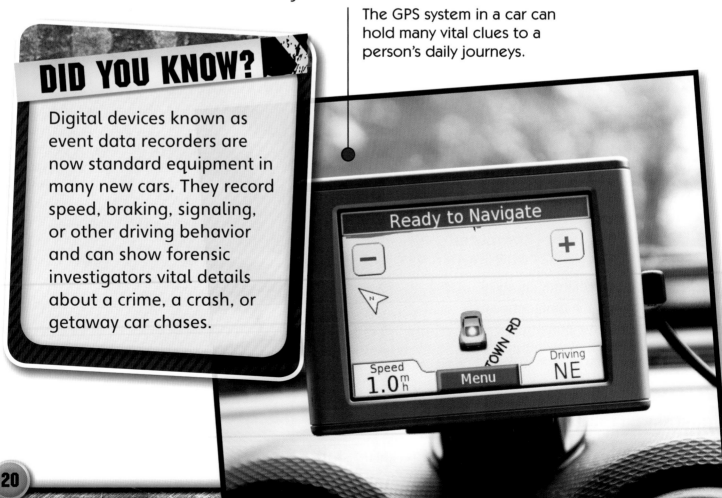

Ready to Navigate

Speed
1.0 m/h

Menu

Driving
NE

# CASE FILE

In 2008, terrorists attacked the Taj Mahal Palace hotel in Mumbai, India. More than 170 people were killed by guns and grenades. After a terrifying gun battle, nine of the terrorist gunmen were killed.

A cell phone and three GPS devices were found in the abandoned vehicles after the attacks. Forensic experts proved the 10 terrorists had traveled from Karachi, Pakistan. Nine of the men were killed in the attack.

One terrorist survived, 22-year-old Mohammad Ajmal Amir Qasab of Pakistan. He faced charges of terrorism, murder, and possessing explosives. The digital evidence from his GPS device helped the police to gather information about the addresses and routes he had taken. He pleaded not guilty before confessing. In 2010, Qasab was convicted of his crimes and sentenced to death.

Fire and smoke poured from the hotel as troops and terrorists carried out a gun battle.

# Cell Phone Secrets

Your cell phone hides many secrets about you. It can trace your movements and even tell forensic scientists if you are a criminal!

## The Spy in Your Pocket

Memory cards in cell phones are packed with information. These include contact lists and messages (including deleted text), calls received and made, and data about where the phone has been used. These details can uncover a criminal's recent history.

## DID YOU KNOW?

To catch criminals from digital evidence, cyber forensic researchers have designed a device called a flasher box. This transfers data from a cell phone to a computer. It helps detectives without any electronic expertise to check for digital clues when trying to solve criminal cases.

The data from a cell phone can be downloaded onto a computer in seconds to reveal vital clues.

# CASE FILE

In 2007, Joe O'Reilly was convicted of murdering his wife Rachel at their home in Dublin, Ireland. Much of the evidence against him came from his cell phone. From his calls, the police determined exactly where O'Reilly was around the time of his wife's murder. Each time a cell phone is used, it connects to a cell tower that serves a specific area. This precise information is recorded inside the phone.

Rachel O'Reilly's badly beaten body was found in 2004. Her husband was eventually jailed for life because of the digital evidence inside his phone.

## Text Evidence

If you think text messages can be anonymous, think again! Experts can study every detail in a text or e-mail to discover who sent it.

In 2005, 19-year-old Jenny Nicholl from Yorkshire, UK, disappeared and was never seen again. David Hodgson had killed her. To make her family think she was still alive, he texted them from Jenny's phone. Forensic **linguists** proved the text messages were not from Jenny but matched the style of 48-year-old Hodgson, a suspect. In 2008, Hodgson was sent to prison for Jenny's murder.

The style of a text message can give clues to the sender's identity.

# Cell Phone Evidence

Two murder cases in the United Kingdom were particularly shocking because the victims were 10-year-old children. Cell phone evidence was used in both trials.

## Schoolboy Attack

In 2000, Damilola Taylor was found bleeding to death in a stairway to apartments in Peckham, London. Forensic scientists believed he had been attacked before falling on a broken bottle. Damilola died from his wounds. Who would attack a 10-year-old on his way home from school?

Two years later, two teenage brothers went on trial for Damilola's murder, but cell phone evidence cleared them of the crime. The judge ruled they could not have killed Damilola because their phones had been used too far from the crime scene. Four years later, the brothers were found guilty in a retrial. Forensic investigators found Damilola's blood on the brothers' clothing.

The death of Damilola Taylor led to a massive police hunt for his killers.

## Missing Girls

In 2002, Holly Wells and Jessica Chapman went out to buy candy in their home town of Soham, UK. They walked past the school caretaker's house where Ian Huntley lived. He invited the girls inside, killed them, and hid their bodies a few miles away.

Local people, including Huntley, helped the police search for the missing girls. Cell phone evidence made the police look more closely at Huntley. Digital forensics showed exactly where and when Jessica's last phone signal had been switched off. It was linked to a cell tower near the caretaker's house. Ian Huntley was eventually convicted of the girls' murder from a variety of evidence and sent to prison for life.

Holly Wells (left) and her best friend Jessica Chapman (right) were tragically murdered in 2002.

## SCIENCE SECRETS

Some forensic scientists warn that although computers and cell phones can hold useful digital evidence, it is not always foolproof. A criminal might have someone else use his phone while he's robbing a bank to give himself an **alibi**!

# Catching Criminals

Computer forensic laboratories across the United States examine thousands of electrical devices every year in the search for criminal evidence. There can be many surprises.

Will these flames destroy the evidence on this hard drive?

## Guilty Secrets

FBI files contain bizarre stories of desperate people who try to destroy digital evidence that might get them into trouble. One report told of a suspect who tried to burn down his house, hoping the flames would destroy his computer hard drive, which held enough evidence to send him to prison. But he failed.

Another man shot a bullet through his computer to destroy the hard drive. However, a second hard drive was full of incriminating evidence, so he went to prison after all. Throwing computers and cell phones into lakes or rivers rarely works. Data is usually waterproof!

# CASE FILE

An armed gang robbed 21 banks in Texas before the FBI caught the five men in 2008. Known as the Scarecrow Bandits, the robbers wore floppy hats and flannel shirts as a form of disguise.

At their trial, cell phone records, recorded conversations, and images from aerial **surveillance** teams were presented as evidence. Digital forensics experts used text messages, photographs, and call logs from the gang's 14 phones to convict the men.

One of the phones was recovered from a sewer after being there for two days—a suspect had tried to flush it down a toilet. Each gang member received a long prison sentence. The leader was sent to prison for 354 years!

## DID YOU KNOW?

Once a sealed cell phone or computer arrives at a secure lab, it is given to a forensic examiner to uncover the data. Video images of crime scenes may also arrive for examination. The latest software can gather a lot of useful information from images recorded on **CCTV** cameras.

Forensic scientists can determine when and where a victim's body fell in the water from the moment his or her cell phone stopped working.

# What Next?

Cyber crime secrets will become even more amazing as technology continues to develop. Cyber criminals and cyber forensics will try to keep one step ahead in the cyber crime race.

## Cyber Spies

Digital CCTV is just one area in which computer scientists are developing new software and high-tech equipment in the fight against crime. Cameras pointing at us in busy airports or public places will soon do more than record fuzzy pictures. New technology will instantly assess threats and warn of crimes about to take place.

CCTV digital technology is always watching us!

## Warning Signs

Intelligent CCTV can detect unusual situations or recognize a suspect in a crowd. This computer vision technology can check for patterns of behavior that may go undetected by humans. If someone is behaving strangely, a computer can assess the situation. If there seems to be a major risk, the police are alerted.

## Matching Faces

The latest high-definition digital CCTV cameras could be used to identify criminals even if they have changed their appearance. Face-recognition technology scans an image of a suspect's face and records accurate measurements, such as the distance between the eyes. This face data can quickly find a match on a database of known criminals. Whatever the future holds, it seems certain that forensic experts will be looking at us more closely.

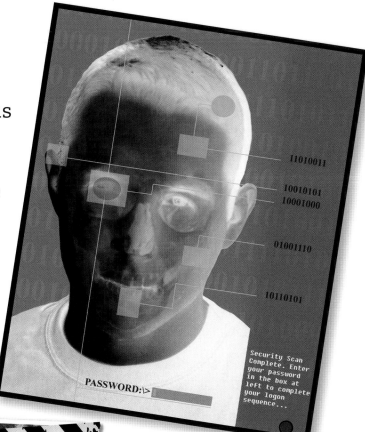

A computer scan of a suspect's face can be matched against police records.

## SCIENCE SECRETS

Intelligent CCTV will soon be listening, too! Computer scientists are developing audio-recognition software to listen for particular sounds, such as screams. The camera will instantly swivel to the direction of the sound and analyze a high-definition image in milliseconds.

# Glossary

**alibi**
proof that someone accused of a crime was at another place during the crime

**Al-Qaeda**
an organization behind some global terrorist attacks, such as those on September 11, 2001, in the U.S.

**bot**
short for robot; This computer program allows an attacker to gain control over affected computers.

**CCTV**
closed-circuit television

**court**
the place where a criminal is questioned and proven innocent or guilty

**CSI**
crime scene investigation

**digital forensics**
the collection and presentation of digitally stored evidence in criminal investigations

**encrypted**
information concealed by means of a code

**evidence**
material presented to a court in a crime case

**firewall**
computer software that prevents access by unauthorized users

**forensic**
scientific methods used to investigate and establish facts in criminal courts

**fraud**
dishonest methods used to cheat someone of something valuable

**GPS device**
global positioning system; GPS devices receive satellite signals to show the location of the device.

**hacking**
illegal access to a computer

**illegal**
against the law

**incriminating**
to show evidence or proof of involvement in a crime

**linguist**
a language specialist

**malware**
malicious software programs designed to damage a computer system

**obscene**
very shocking
and offensive

**Pentagon**
the main building
of the U.S. Defense
Department in
Washington, D.C.

**phishing**
sending e-mails with
links to fake web site
pages to fool users
into giving out
personal details

**PIN**
personal
identification
number

**predator**
someone who
bullies, victimizes,
or preys on another

**ransom**
something paid
or demanded for
the freedom of a
captured person

**spammer**
someone who sends
unwanted e-mails
to a large number
of e-mail addresses

**spyware**
technology that
helps to find
information about
people without
their knowledge

**surveillance**
keeping a
close watch

**suspect**
someone thought
to be guilty of
a crime

**suspended sentence**
a prison sentence
that does not take
effect immediately
unless the criminal
offends again

**trojan**
a seemingly useful
computer program
that contains
instructions that
cause damage

**warrant**
a legal document
that gives a police
officer the power to
carry out the law

**worm**
a harmful computer
program that sends
copies of itself
to attack other
computers on
a network

# Index

bots  12

CCTV  27, 28, 29
cell phone  4, 5, 13, 21, 22, 23, 24, 25, 26, 27
computer  4, 5, 6, 7, 8, 9, 11, 12, 13, 14, 15, 16, 17, 18, 19, 22, 25, 26, 27, 28, 29
computer virus  5, 6, 7, 12
court 5, 16
crime scene  4, 5, 6, 14, 20, 24, 27
cyber thieves  8, 9, 10, 11, 12, 13

digital forensics 4, 12, 17 25, 27
digital information  4, 5, 16, 20, 27

e-mails  5, 6, 10, 11, 15, 23
evidence  4, 5, 13, 14, 15, 16, 18, 19, 20, 21, 22, 23, 24, 25, 26, 27

FBI  5, 9, 15, 26, 27
firewall  7
fraud  5, 10, 11, 12, 13

GPS device  20, 21

hacking  5, 6, 7, 8, 9, 12, 13, 14
Huntley, Ian  25

identity theft  12
Internet  5, 6, 7, 10, 13, 15, 19

malware  6
McGuire, Melanie  18, 19

phishing  10, 11

security  5, 8, 14
software  6, 7, 9, 11, 17, 27, 28, 29
spam  10, 11, 12
spyware  7

Taylor, Damilola  24
terrorism  12, 14, 15, 21
text messages  5, 22, 23, 27
trojan  7

vandal  6, 7, 8

worm  7

# Web Finder

http://computer.howstuffworks.com/worst-computer-viruses.htm
Learn about some of the worst computer viruses of all time.

http://investigation.discovery.com/videos/solved-computer-forensics.html
This short video shows how computer forensics helped to convict Melanie McGuire.

http://investigation.discovery.com/videos/solved-cell-phone-tracking.html
This short video shows how cell phone evidence can help trace a killer.

http://www.justice.gov/criminal/cybercrime/rules/kidinternet.htm
This U.S. Department of Justice site provides "what would you do" scenarios regarding cyber ethics, rules, and hacking.

www.mcgruffspo.com/cybersafetysat.cfm
Use this poster to help protect yourself and others from cyber crime.